Celebrating the Quaker Way

Ben Pink Dandelion

For all of us

Second edition

Second edition,

Published May 2010 by Quaker Books,

Friends House, 173 Euston Road, London NW1 2BJ

www.quaker.org.uk

Enquiries should be addressed to Quaker Books,
Quaker Communications, Friends House, 173 Euston Road,
London NW1 2BJ

www.quaker.org.uk

ISBN 978 1 907123 13 9

Foreword

The trustees of The Joseph Rowntree Charitable Trust have commissioned this short devotional work to help us describe and celebrate the Quaker way that we know and practise in Britain Yearly Meeting, and which is practised elsewhere. This is a form of worship which is sometimes termed 'liberal' or 'unprogrammed', to distinguish it from evangelical or programmed worship found in other parts of the world; however the heart of this book is for all those who enjoy open worship as part of their Quaker experience and who seek to live their lives as Friends.

It is a Quaker way that we are familiar with, and from which we derive great strength, comfort and challenge, but one that is hard to describe. We feel it draws us together, closer to God and to God's purposes, giving us a place to stand, an understanding of how to live our lives. What we share together goes deeper than words.

But it is vital that we find these words – for our own clarity of understanding, for the enlightenment of others and for the growth of our meetings. Where we should be eloquent, we often find ourselves tongue-tied. In a religious society without trained ministers, the task of attempting to speak what we know and understand of the nature and purposes of God falls to each one of us, not just a few. It is something we all need to encourage in each other.

We are deeply grateful for what Ben has produced. What he has written comes to us in his own voice, and the voices of Friends he has spoken to. We offer it in the hope that it will be widely read, and will inspire each of us to find our own voice, to speak passionately to each other of what we know, to express the power we find in the experience of our Quaker faith, to be God's ministers in the world today.

Marion McNaughton
Chair of Trustees
Joseph Rowntree Charitable Trust

Introduction

This pocket-sized book celebrates the Quaker way and affirms the wonderful riches of the Quaker tradition in Britain, and the Quaker 'Liberal tradition' more widely. It is a book for Quakers rather than about them. It talks of 'us' and 'we' and is for 'insiders'. It is a devotional book, for us.

I talk of God in the way Friends have traditionally talked of the divine, although some today may prefer other terms, and I hope that those readers can 'translate' or hear where the words come from, as they might approach ministry in meeting for worship. I write as a Quaker who came to meeting as an atheist/agnostic, drawn in by the peace testimony, an ex-anarchist, happy to find another place without leaders and without votes. Two years in, I had an experience aboard a Greyhound bus in America that gave me a sense of being lifted up, held, and since then perpetually accompanied by what I call God, but which I know is ultimately a mystery that it is not for me to know too closely. Thus, my being a Quaker moved from a primarily political affiliation to a place where I could connect and reconnnect with that grace-filled sense of being watched over, guarded and guided. It has fitted me not only intellectually but practically in my life of faith. It gives me exactly the form of worship and the opportunity for expression and service that matches my own experience of direct inward encounter.

We all have a ministry, or a series of ministries, each for its season, where we use the spiritual gifts given us by God. This book is written as part of my ministry. It draws on my Quaker experience, all I have heard and read in these last decades, and some twenty conversations conducted especially for the book (these Friends' words are in quotation marks). I trust I have been faithful to what has been given me.

I begin by suggesting what it means to call ourselves Quaker. The second part is more reflective, and I celebrate the nature of silent worship and its transforming potential, vocal ministry, discernment, and community. In the third part I explore the call to action following on from our direct relationship with God, our 'testimony'.

1 I am a Quaker

I am a Quaker. I am part of a worldwide Quaker community and I inhabit that knowledge daily. It helps me live the way I want to. The knowledge and reality of that community membership informs my life and gives me the strength I need to live faithfully, to speak truth to power, to witness in the world.

I feel different from those around me, and my faith impels me to live a different life from the one the secular world tells me I should. As I walk down the street, catch the bus, take the train, drive, eat, speak, or buy, I am not following society's norms, but those alternative ones hewn out by Quakers over three and a half centuries of discerning what is called from us as a people of God. I feel clothed in my faith.

That witness is not about hats and tithes now, but it is still about not deferring to those in positions of power, about treating all of humanity equally, about not supporting institutions that perpetuate wrong thinking or wrongdoing. It is about speaking out and living 'out' for justice and peace, and the integrity of creation.

Our testimony is about simplicity over commercialism, materialism and greed. It is about having what we need rather than what we want. It is about the integrity of all over hierarchy and competition and the exploitation of people for profit. It is about promoting peace, not war. It is about not seeing war as a means to any end. It is about community, not individualism. It is about stewardship, not short-term gain. It is all about living faithfully, not for ourselves but for the greater good. Testimony is about attempting God's will. It is about living a life for justice in the world, not only among us. And as Quakers, wonderfully, we do not have to do these things alone.

Our Quaker identity and community supports us when we are in the world and countering its assumptions, and it informs and changes our lives. It helps me in the stands I want to make and it helps me see others I should be making. A core set of values and principles travels with me and through me, so that my life may preach. I am given support and inspiration, aspiration and affirmation.

When I am wrestling with an issue, I can take it to my Quaker friends, my Quaker network, my Quaker meeting. I can seek 'clearness' informally or formally. I can help others 'discern'. I can find help interpreting my sense of what God wants of me, and what that may mean in any particular situation. My knowledge of the presence of such a community in itself gives support and guidance. The well-known stories of Quaker action in the world, of reaction to the unforeseen, of resolve against the odds, of response to the dangerous and hostile, give me tools to mould and shape my own responses. I am both held by the community and am part of the holding – holding others as they discern, holding the tradition as we discern, holding the future of the Quaker way in a group that has no leaders but ourselves, no 'them' but us.

And I know that this desire to get my life right is a priority for me, but also is a shared priority. I know that others will listen to learn, and share what they already know so that I may learn. For all of us, these things matter enormously. We are friends as well as Friends, and we are friends with the shared purpose and desire to get our lives right.

This friendship transcends geography. It is wider than my immediate neighbourhood, stretches farther than my meeting's boundary, beyond the confines of any one yearly meeting and any one language. My Quaker belonging is about being part of a global network of those I have met, sat on committees with, worshipped with, discerned with. We have worked together and prayed together. We have washed pots, raked leaves, sat in meetings for hours or committees for days. We have known each other in the things which have felt eternal, as well as those things which truly are. We have slept on floors in meeting houses as Young Friends, stayed up all night talking excitedly, experimented with worship, and had our hearts linked and broken along the way. We have travelled to visit each other, knowing that we will find a welcome and a like mind at the end of the journey. We have known that, as long as we stay within the Quaker fold, we will most likely meet again. It is a companionship of the greatest depth and trust. These are friendships 'for life' in every sense.

Often nothing needs to be spoken. Silently, we share a reaction to a news item, to a beggar in the street, to a billboard advertisement, or to a choice of product in a supermarket.

At other times, we can joyfully disagree and argue in love to see the other's view, to decide together what it is best to do. We may continue to disagree, but most often what is shared outweighs what is not. We are able to continue living alongside one another 'up the mountain' of our collective affiliation to the Religious Society of Friends.

All the time, we are galvanised more and more to action. The repeated urgings of the faithful Friend, the mailings from Yearly Meeting, or an article in the Quaker press at any point may strike the seasoned nerve, and move us from concern to action. After one successful demonstration, the next feels all the easier. We become old hands at being creative in our dealings with the establishment. We drive food aid to refugees, blockade nuclear bases, worship outside early warning defence establishments, petition and lobby, talk and persuade. And even when we are not successful at this moment, the seed can be planted from which the next generation can draw nourishment and support.

We, as Quakers, have long traditions of work against slavery and for penal reform started by pioneers amongst us, those who were not always listened to, but who nevertheless created a legacy we have been able to join and follow. If we are not listened to today, we can have the hope that we may be pioneers for tomorrow's Quakers.

We know we may not be right, but we also know that what matters most is the faithful seeking that informs all we do. We do not always have the solutions, but we know we are sometimes given 'incredible answers' to questions we have. When we come together, we find community and acceptance in our worship and together discern dreams we never imagined we could have, and ones we never could have had on our own. In that place of holy discovery, beyond reason, we can find divinely inspired solutions that we could never have found by logic alone. Such is the art of discernment, the art of the holy.

We know for ourselves that we have found a spiritual community that is the best place for us to sit within for now. For many of us, it has been a 'homecoming'. It is a place for us to live our lives, to position our lives within this tradition and all its insights, and a place from which to continue our journey. It is not a place that claims to have all the answers but one which rather encourages questions. It is a spiritual home which emphasises seeking and which is cautious about finally finding. It is a spiritual home which encourages us to make our own choices, to live by our own interpretations of the tradition and its current understandings, a place to work out for ourselves what a Quaker life may look like.

It gives us the tradition to guide us, that legacy of past understandings, and a set of amazing tools to help us get it right for now: worship; an understanding of worshipping community; a discernment process; and, ultimately, the ability to make whatever we will of what we have, to become whoever we choose to be as a people of faith regardless of the past or present.

This freedom is also a responsibility, and it is right and wonderful that we undertake this journey together. 'I am a Quaker' is not an individualistic statement, it is a declaration of community. It is to declare our spiritual values, here and now in this community, and our endeavour to live a life within and alongside those values. It is to discern within and against the tradition. What a wonderful gift it is to be a Quaker.

2 Meeting

Worship

Come into the silence of a Quaker meeting. Outward quiet gives us the inward place of amazing opportunity and fantastical connection. 'Sink down to the seed' and we find we inhabit a new space, out of 'the world', away from the earthly and secular, that touches heaven and allows us to find and feel God. Absence leads to Presence. This is an intentional silence, a deliberate attempt to feel connection, additional to the incidental divine accompaniment we can feel at any time in any week.

We sit in a tradition of revolutionary discovery: a discovery of the power found within the silence that transforms lives, that transforms communities of believers, that transforms the world through the call to action that emerges within that inward relationship.

What happens to us in the silence varies but we know its power and its value. We know that it works, that it gives us a doorway into the mystery of faith. We know that the unique Quaker form of worship is the place, the wonderful place, we find we need to be.

The silence of worship is not just an absence of noise, or even an outward stilling of the physical, it is a journey within, a 'going inside' to a deeply felt but easily reached place of holy relationship. Together, we meet each other in the silence, come together, 'all focusing on something we share', 'picking up the same questions in the silence', gathered, before God. We come expectantly and in surrender. We come in the hope of we know not what, the hope of faith. We come in the humility of those seeking, those grateful for what we are given, those hungry to hear the call, those eager to work with God to further God's loving purposes. We come as those who know that the world is not as loving as it might be, that humanity hurts itself as well as the planet, that we need to at least try doing our bit to help, and that our faith both requires this of us, and helps us achieve what we discern is best.

We come too with our own sense of brokenness, of shortcomings, and failures and fallings short. We come with our own need to be in right relationship with each other and with the divine, our own need of help and accompaniment. We come with our own desire to feel again and again the magic and grace of God's love in our lives, of God's wisdom alongside our thinking, of God's faith in us as we struggle from time to time with our faith in God or in ourselves.

Thus our times of worship, whether alone at home or at meeting, feed us and our faith while also representing our response to the mystery of the divine. We sit in the silence, open to God and opening to God. God is there and we continue the silence in awe and wonder, in adoring prayer and gratitude for all we have been given. We 'bathe in the silence' and it 'feels right, just right'.

'A few weeks ago, I wasn't well enough to come. Come the hour, I sat down and thought "I'm going to sit here quietly, this is my hour when I should be at meeting" and I was alone, but I sat quietly, just emptied my mind, and suddenly I didn't feel alone, I was sure there was something happening at meeting and I felt it, and I didn't feel alone for that hour, I was greatly comforted.'

The beauty of silence is that it allows us to engage where we are. We are not dovetailed into someone else's sermon, neither are our devotions determined by an outward liturgy. Rather, our motions of faith can sit where they need to be, close to us in their authenticity and sincerity, closer to God in their directness and individuality. 'Let Love be the first motion': the motivating and originating love of our outward life and witness sits as a reflection of our impulse towards love within. It is a personal motion of love, for ourselves, for our friends, for God, for the 'complete place' of unity with the divine that we discover in that inward and outward silence.

We review our lives. We pray. We hold in the Light. We think. We feel connected, refreshed, accepted. We walk with our guide. We hand things over to God. We trust. We find faith need not be total. We see that hope is more important than belief. We feel. We go beyond reason, to where it feels as if the whole of life is God. We find nothing between us and God. Life becomes prayer.

I write as if this encounter with God and personal transformation is automatic and easy. It is not, of course, and many of us sit in meeting still hoping to feel God's presence. Maybe we have, and have not recognised it. Maybe God's invitation has not yet come to us. Between those moments of gathered intensity, we learn, sometimes painfully, to wait hopefully and expectantly. As Quakers, as part of a tradition founded and sustained on direct inward encounter, we know that an experience of the divine can and does come regularly to thousands of Friends. That knowledge may not make it easier for those of us still seeking, but it can turn a potentially pessimistic and cynical atheism into an optimistic agnosticism. Believing it is worth seeking was the original impulse that led George Fox not only to his despair but also to his critical experience of encounter and truth.

For some of us, often it is outside of meeting that God feels closest, or that we feel more 'in the right place with God'. I call these times 'holy moments', when everything feels aligned and congruent. For me, they have often come walking the streets of London, where the aesthetic of the outward architecture, the richness of life on the street around me, the delicacy of the cuisine on offer, or the arc of a particularly graceful classic motor car, calls forth the joy and thanksgiving deep within my soul at being a part of this holy landscape. Indeed, given my perpetual sense of accompaniment and the joy that goes with it, I feel God close at hand almost everywhere I choose to be truly open.

Going to meeting, then, is about intentionality and about communal sacramental connection. There, I join with others to experience 'communion after the manner of Friends'. It is powerful and wonderful. It is the inward supper. There is something very important and precious about the regularity and routine of the discipline of deliberateness. It is a discipline of remaining aware of the relationship with God, of putting it first, of knowing that, particularly when it feels least helpful, or when we feel least deserving, this time of intentional expectancy, and the hope that underpins it, is exactly what is required.

There is something to be treasured in the routines and rituals of Quaker meeting. There is familiarity but also the remembrance to ourselves of the desire to set time aside to concentrate on what is alongside us at all times but often hidden from us by our busyness. 'Keeping the pace' as well as the peace of our lives does not override the need to deliberately give ourselves times of intentional intimacy with God. 'My Quakerism lives in my local meeting – always the place I come back to, and want to come back to.'

Ministry

The direct relationship we experience with God leads to a continued spiritual intimacy. Nobody and nothing needs to be between ourselves and the divine: we are all raised up to work alongside and for God's loving purposes in and over 'the world.' Each of us is a precious child of God and is given ministry, a spiritual gift or gifts to share freely and faithfully with and beyond the community. Quaker faith is about doing and not just being. It may begin with the individual but it is never private.

Silence within the Quaker setting is used for the approach to God but also as the medium for discerning the action we are called to take individually and corporately. In and through the silence, we are gathered and guided by God. Wary of explicit theology, we make silence our approach to God and also our response, a symbol of our particular attitude towards not knowing, or feeling not able to say too much in particular, about the mystery of the divine.

Cautious about speech, we are concerned that our attempts to transmit something of our experience fall short or demean the experience we are trying to convey. We meet in silence, discern and offer ministry, and let it be received in silence. It may look like an arid loop but it rests totally on the unmediated experience of the divine, unbidden but continually available, the personal and corporate discernment of that experience, and ministry in silence as well as speech. Ministry may be given in 'entire and trustful silence alone'; words may be unnecessary to convey what God is giving us to share. Equally, others sometimes speak exactly what is on our hearts.

Vocal ministry is different from everyday talk. Ministry may be 'more eloquent than everyday speech' or feel very specific: 'there is a pounding, shaking, I feel forced – my voice disappears, I have only the vaguest idea of what I am going to say, only a vague idea of what I've said'; 'something stays in my head, won't go away, then an angle on it will come, then the words – it becomes very difficult to breathe, but I say it and calm down, nothing comes in afterwards, very often I don't remember what was said.'

'Just thinking about it makes me shake … I feel terrified, … it's exposing yourself … exhilarating but also terrifying … if I had a choice, I would stay sat down.'

We are vessels. It is not our ministry but we need to be faithful to the leadings we are given. 'Water tastes of the pipes – vocal ministry works with my experience but comes through me.'

We are not islands, neither should we try to be for little do we know the consequences and impact of our own actions. When we are advised to come to meeting regardless of how we feel, that sage advice is not just for our own welfare but for whosoever we may meet that day. The ministry we are led to give may not be for us or even the majority of the meeting, yet the 'wonderful book of discipline' reminds us that it may be for somebody. I once heard as a 'ministry' someone advertise a video they had been involved in producing. They even gave the price and how to order it. On my high Quaker horse, I sat there amazed at what might count as ministry, and then was chastened by a flow of the most unexpectedly insightful and powerful ministry, all springing from the video being about bereavement, and the word having found life in the silence of meeting.

Whether or not we minister vocally in meeting, we all have a ministry. To say we have a gift or a particular ministry is to say nothing at all about our human self but merely to reflect on something given us by God for a purpose: 'ministry is a gift to me to share with the meeting'. As it says in 1 Corinthians 12, we all have different gifts and we all have our part to play. The test of authenticity is found in the fruits of the spirit and in the building of community.

In a permissive Quakerism, we decide what is appropriate, what is Quaker for us, how we interpret our Quaker faith in day-to-day life. We no longer look and sound different from the rest of the population, as the earlier Friends did with their Quaker grey and insistence on 'thee' and 'thou', numbering days and months instead of using their pagan names. The sense of difference between us and those whose behaviours we wish to challenge, as with our faith, is now an inward affair. And so, equally, is the challenge, to live that difference inwardly, to 'know' it intimately and to live our lives in that spirit, still as co-agents with God.

Discernment

In a faith which claims God speaks to us directly, knowing what is of God is crucial and we require reliable access to that experience for guidance in daily life.

In practice, we come to know what is in 'right ordering' within our lives, perhaps through finding we have got things wrong, or feeling the fruits of the spirit that emerge, ultimately developing a sense of alignment or congruence or 'instinct' when we are getting it right.

It may mean we need to 'find somewhere quiet and stop'. 'Home becomes a place of prayer – I open the curtains with a prayer, wake up in the night with a prayer … have a cup of tea with God.' 'I pray about all decisions and get to a picture, an image, … sometimes just become clear having prayed about it.' There is a sense of 'flow' or 'energy' when we have clarity, and one of being 'out of kilter' when we do not.

We can all encounter God directly. We can all experience God's guidance and we can all minister that to the group. We use the same basis for our business meetings: expectant waiting and ministry which comes out of the silence. It is worship with a theme, and for some of us, Quaker business method is the most visible and reliable symbol of direct encounter. In one committee there have been 'lots of practical things to do but they are interspersed with an explicit feeling that what we are doing is God's work.' Yearly Meeting with its gatherings of over one thousand Friends is particularly affirming of our faith and practice. Large numbers of us regularly and reliably find a 'sense of the meeting' and we move forward on major decisions. We are well practised at discernment and it is a communal gift we should celebrate more explicitly.

So discernment, deciding what is of God and what is not, is the most visible role of the gathered meeting but also its most fundamental. It is the most crucial exercise of a church which claims its authority and wisdom is found in corporate direct encounter over and against text or tradition. The gathered meeting decides for itself what is truly from God, no book, leader, or part of the past. Our future is in our discernment.

Community

Quakerism has never been about going it alone. Numbers bring reliability in terms of Quaker discernment and political strength in trying to change the world, but there is something more fundamental in being 'gathered as in a net', the human desire and need to relate. I have talked with ex-Quakers, many of whom still feel they are Quaker but that the local or national meeting has lost its Quaker way. There is nowhere else for these grieving Quakers to go and so many sit at home and worship on their own. No one can test their leadings or unite with their concerns. No one is there to accompany them on their faith journey, to be alongside, to help with pastoral needs or the nurture of their ministry, other than God alone. This I suggest is not how God or Quakerism imagines a life of faith. Rather, community is at the heart of Quaker worship and of Quaker discernment. We don't need to be all in the same place for prayer and worship to feel powerfully connected but knowing when others are also engaged in these ways can have a great effect.

'People praying on a topic is powerful, not physically together but wherever they are, we don't need our bodies to be in the same place … I learn and relearn about faith, I really need not to worry, to trust in God, and give it to God and not grab it back … just trust that the right thing will happen.'

Our structures reflect and nurture this joint dependence on each other and on God. We are all spiritually equal, all part of the 'priesthood'. We can all attend business meetings and should do. We share the tasks that need to be done to remain an effective worship group, and rotate them. We are all responsible financially. We are all responsible practically. We are all responsible spiritually, all elders and overseers to each other and the meeting, all nurturing and caring for the community.

Often it is the less formal moments that build community most. My meeting has loved its days of bench-waxing or railing-painting, and in a previous meeting regular day-long walks attracted not only a high proportion of those who turn up on Sunday but their non-Quaker family and friends. Having fewer named posts in my meeting has helped more people to come forward, and reminds me of the meeting in Chicago where, in crisis over nominations, they scrapped all the formal structure and began again with a list of immediate needs. Volunteers come forward when the tasks have life: 'The Holy Spirit took me by the hand'. We are bound together by the processes and the fruits of our discernment.

Our worship witnesses to the radical and unique form of Quaker liturgy, an unmediated and direct alternative within a religious world still dominated by the rule of expertise, ministers and mediators, personal and textual authority. Quaker business meeting witnesses to the power of collective spiritual experience in seeking God's guidance on any matter.

The minutes and epistles that emerge from these meetings are witness not only to their content but to a process that continues to subvert the secular hierarchies of the status quo. The book of discipline, reviewed in each generation, is testimony to the Quaker search for truth, the experience of continuing revelation, and that God requires us to take on new roles and emphases in each age. All witness to our rich corporate tradition and that we are, powerfully and practically, Quakers together.

3　Testimony

The direct encounter with the mystery of the divine at the heart of Quaker faith demands not only the response of worship and continued expectant waiting but an active demonstration of the insights God gives us. In other words, we are not given guidance that is private only to us either in its scope or in its application. Faith is about action in the world.

This witness to God's imperatives working through us has been traditionally labelled by Quakers as 'testimony'. What we call a testimony to the grace of God in the life of a deceased Friend is our witness to that grace which was so obvious in how they lived.

Similarly as our lives preach of God's loving purposes and work towards their fulfilment, so that witness is referred to as our testimony.

Today we may see our place in the world as less problematic than the first Quakers did in the seventeenth century, and may feel our faith and our Quakerism as optional, non-essential preferences rather than prerequisites for a faithful life. However, even from this perspective, we sit within a tradition which has always refused to be confined to collective devotions without effects beyond the meeting house. It is not about having a spiritual life with consequences, it is about the spiritual life containing within it the response of prayer within worship and prayerful practice outside of formal worship: our Quaker faith has always understood itself as being about the whole of life. 'I cannot separate my life from being a Quaker.'

'I am a Quaker, completely, I don't think of it as a belief, it is just the way that I am, it's how I am, … it's my identity, it is not about deciding you're a Quaker, it is about realising you're a Quaker.'

Even as we are left to choose how to interpret what our Quaker faith may look like most of the time, it is still a task we have to face. So, in our daily lives we may live in smaller houses than our peers, drive smaller cars or none at all, and own fewer things. We may be invisible as Quakers in a landscape of increasing consumer and environmental awareness but are highly self-aware and self-questioning. And our fundamental reasons for our Quaker concerns are spiritually based, not born out of secular humanism. My own Quaker life now contains within it many of the concerns and consequences of my earlier life as an anarchist but now I act out of God's love within me, not a secular celebration of a particular ideology. It is not about acting now for this life is all we have, but acting now because it is God's time to act, for my generation and the next.

It is about our lives being ones of 'becoming'. We are never just a Quaker (as others are not just a Muslim) but we are striving always to be the better person of faith, the more obedient, the more faithful, the more aware. Faith is about becoming. 'Peace starts with us – I am the only person I can change … God works with us as individual souls.' We work on our lives, 'letting the Light in, not dwelling on the darkness' and we support each other: 'to be out there in the world doing this as a small group is hard, knowing that you're not wasting your time or dwelling on irrelevancies.' Some of us feel we don't easily fit into society. Not coming to meeting can increase that sense of alienation or make us less thoughtful in our choices. Coming to meeting can make us more aware of 'problems and injustices' but also give us support to do the things we feel we need to.

This sense of always 'becoming' is simply a fact of God's invitation in our lives. We are not Quakers because we are good, but because we are not. God loves us in spite of ourselves and we respond because of how we are. And we become more towards on our journey of faith. More congruent.

And, as Jesus' teachings tell us, worry does not add one moment to our life, one measure to our life's journey. Worry is the opposite of faith. It is focused on particulars, built on notions, and has no room for the spectacular and that which is not yet known, the focus of hope in Romans 8. Faith takes us we know not where but the destination is unimportant, the process of being led and following faithfully is all. God will take us where we need to go and 'the big picture will emerge in time', a glimpse or reflection of the republic of heaven. Worry takes up energy and time so much more usefully spent on the fruits of discipleship, testimony to the grace of God acting in our lives now and calling us out to help others and to help create a just and peaceful world.

Quakers 'celebrate life, life as it can be for everybody.' We have 'a way of life, not a religion' and we 'have to be prepared to live it, to keep it in mind all the time.' There is so much to celebrate: 'sincerity, the involvement of everybody', 'the respect given children', 'testimony and the expectations and values that go with that, silence, meeting, worship, the direct line to God, that questions are okay, encouraged'. We are part of a tradition of people trying to achieve greater justice in the world and we have also had great moments of corporate insight and action that spur us on in our present-day attempts to change the world. And taking action is simple.

'Our meeting had received an appeal for work with children in Madagascar and we were oohing and aahing about whether to send money and how much and then Gabriel, seven, ministered. He suggested the children's meeting could bake biscuits and sell them to help send money to the children. This has now become a regular activity but part of our meeting life still led by the young people.'

The emphasis of our testimony today is on justice through simplicity and moderation, peace, integrity, care of creation, and the nurture of community. Testimony is expression. Quakers are not 'for peace' but rather know, in the deepest sense of the word, that peace is a holy imperative as part of a just society. We do not prefer peace or campaign for peace in isolation from a whole lot of other issues, rather we have imbibed God's loving purposes in their simplicity and totality. We inhabit our testimony. It is both straightforward and enormously far-reaching. It is simple but total. It is, as it always has been for Quakers, about turning the world upside down. We never forget that: we cannot sit in our meetings without taking on the world and values that lie beyond and against our experience of God.

It is not ultimately about words but about experience. Our testimony is what we do from our experience of God, not what we say. Testimony is not creed but action. This is the same as faith because the two are inseparable. Testimony is only faith in action. It is all of our lives as well as all those things we do together as Quakers. It is wonderfully simple and simply wonderful.

We are Quakers.

Reflection and discussion

The following questions are designed to help you reflect on your own experience of what you value and celebrate about being a Quaker.

They can be used either for individual reflection, or by small groups. If you are meeting as a group, agree some ground rules at the beginning. Important ones might be to allow everyone a chance to speak, to speak only from your own experience, and that no-one has to speak if they don't want to.

Make sure that the book and the questions are accessible to anyone not able to read print, either by obtaining an audio version or reading relevant sections aloud in the group.

If the group is large, you may wish to spend some time in twos, threes or fours before returning to the large group.

Choose between worship sharing or group discussion. Groups may prefer one or the other. Some dislike the discipline of worship sharing when they are bursting with ideas; some find it difficult to contribute to a discussion if they are not given a specific space to do so. Be sensitive to everyone's needs.

Questions for reflection and celebration

1. What do you celebrate about being a Quaker?

2. What are the gifts given to you? What is your unique role in your Quaker community? What is your ministry? How do you affirm it?

3. How can we nurture openness to the magic and grace of God's love in our Meetings?

4. What dreams can we discern for the future? What is your vision for the future of Quaker community? What is the next step for you towards this vision?

5. What is your experience of discernment? What moves you from concern to action? In what ways is your life one of 'becoming'?

6. How do we live our Quakerism more overtly? How do we realise 'the kingdom' in our lives? With others? In our Meetings? In the wider community?

Milton Keynes UK
Ingram Content Group UK Ltd.
UKHW021352260524
443099UK00015B/562

Living the Quaker Way

Ben Pink Dandelion

For all of us

First published May 2012

Quaker Books, Friends House, 173 Euston Road, London
NW1 2BJ

Enquiries should be addressed to the Publications Manager,
Quaker Books, Friends House, 173 Euston Road, London
NW1 2BJ.

www.quaker.org.uk

ISBN 978 1 907123 27 6

Introduction

This pocket-sized book is a companion volume to *Celebrating the Quaker Way*, which first appeared in 2009. The aim of that volume, as its title suggests, was to celebrate the wonderful riches of our Quaker tradition. When in drafts I strayed from celebration to explanation, my editors kindly scored through the offending text, allowing the end product to remain purely a celebratory text for all of us who enjoy the Quaker way.

This book contains explanation. It explores why we do the things we do in the way that we do them. It is still celebratory but also looks at why and how we live our Quaker faith. It is a book about us and for us, based on the Quaker way in Britain. I have tried to keep history to a minimum as we have our own reasons for our present-day faith and practice. It talks of 'us' and 'we' and is for 'insiders'. It is a devotional book, for us.

As I wrote in the earlier book, "I talk of God in the way Friends have traditionally talked of the Divine, although some today may prefer other terms, and I hope that those readers can 'translate' or hear where the words come from, as they might approach ministry in meeting for worship. I write as a Quaker who came to meeting as an atheist/agnostic, drawn in by the peace testimony, an ex-anarchist, happy to find another place without leaders and without votes. Two years in, I had an experience aboard a Greyhound bus in America that gave me a sense of being lifted up, held, and since then perpetually accompanied by what I call God, but which I know is ultimately a mystery that is not for me to know too closely. Thus, Quakerism moved for me from being a primarily political affiliation to a place where I could connect and reconnnect with that grace-filled sense of being watched over, guarded and guided. It has fitted me not only intellectually but practically in my life of faith. It gives me exactly the form of worship and the opportunity for expression and service that matches my own experience of direct inward encounter".

We all have a ministry, or a series of ministries, each for its season, where we use the spiritual gifts given us by God. This book is written as part of my ongoing ministry. It draws on my experience of Quakerism, and extracts from Friends talking on these topics recorded for the book (these Friends' words are in quotation marks). I hope I have been faithful to what has been given me, a twig on the ocean.

The book is divided into three sections. The first is about the inward nature of Quaker spirituality. The second is about the way this informs how we worship and the way we conduct our business through worship. The third part is on how the boundlessness of God's invitation to all of us dramatically affects our view of our neighbours, and of how we are to live in and with 'the world' (the non-Quaker society we are a part of, but so often informed by a different set of values).

Questions on each section for personal reflection and to encourage discussion in our meetings complete the book.

I thank Woodbrooke Quaker Study Centre in Birmingham and my family for giving me the space and encouragement to write this, participants in the November 2011 Pendle Hill course 'And then I heard a voice' for their support and input, and those who read earlier drafts and gave me so much help.

4

1 Inward spirituality

We are Quakers. We worship in a way different from those around us and often our lives feel particular too. For some of us our experience of worship leads to our lifestyle, for others our lifestyle is affirmed by what we find in the silence. For others still, both combine.

Whether our Quaker life is fired from a sense of presence or by a sense of how to live in the world, the foundational Quaker insight is that this 'knowing' is experienced inwardly. It is a knowing of the heart, not the head. We need no outward guides, people or text to lead us into this place of encounter and understanding. Instead we rely particularly on outward absence to release us to a sense of inward presence. We find stillness and silence the best preparation for and the best means to a deeper experience of the spiritual life. Set free and cast away from the world and its concerns, we come to navigate layers of silence to reach towards the mystery and unknowability of God. We sink down within ourselves to find that which we cannot ever fully fathom. We engage in expectant waiting and listening.

Quaker founder George Fox had his first sense of encounter in 1647 when "my hopes in all men were gone" and "I had nothing outwardly to help me". Then he heard a voice, which told him that there was "one, even Christ Jesus" that could speak to his condition, and his "heart did leap for joy". Fox learnt first-hand, as generations of us have since, that having nothing outwardly to help us opens the way to the draught of God's love. God comes to us in the silence and the stillness, and in that place of inward quiet we come to experience God and hear what God is calling us to. The outward is not just unnecessary but also unhelpful. "I've found that [education and learning] is a deceptive path . . . It doesn't really lead to any depth. The Quaker way . . . helps you sink deeper into a way of knowing that moves you out of a rational realm into a deeper way of knowing. It's threatening; I like my false sense of security [but] . . . I try to just let go and surrender . . . I sense that it's right . . . and the Quaker path gives you space to do that."

Many of us are alive with a sense of God's love even amidst busy and noisy lives. We find a holy pace and a small, still centre is present even when all is outwardly elsewhere. God's accompaniment can be wonderfully persistent throughout all kinds of hubbub and thicken even through slumber. "Sometimes I'm called into worship in the middle of the night. I bundle up, go downstairs, and settle into worship. Recently, after a workshop about God's presence, I returned home and had this sense I needed to sit in worship. I got a really clear sense that to change my outward life I had to accept the grace within."

Silence comes easily and naturally to us and we have persisted with it as the basis for worship for over 350 years because it works. The postcard reads "I am a Quaker – in case of emergency, please be quiet". Faced with crisis, we fall to silence. We turn to God to ask for help. Silence is how we approach the Divine collectively, how in those intentional and together-hoped-for moments of sacramental encounter we choose to pray and listen and rest awhile in the tenderness of God's love. "For years, I thought an encounter with the Divine would be huge, a big experience, and that everything would be suddenly clear, but what I've discovered is that simply being faithful day after day boosts the still small voice – there are no cymbals, no thunder."

We know, in both head and heart, that we do not need a minister to preach to us. We have no need to all sing together, or take part in any outward ritual. Those things may help us prepare for the communion we find in the silence, as they do for Quakers in other parts of the world, but are only ever the means to prepare for encounter, not the encounter itself. "We are called to be naked in our worship, both free from our earthly concerns and without the ritual and forms that some in other Churches rely upon." There is no need to mark outwardly what is felt so keenly within. There is no need for outward remembrance of something not forgotten. When we know 'of God', we know of the Divine directly and unforgettably. We know inwardly at both a personal and collective level. "I will never be alone again."

∝

Importantly, this approach to God is available to everyone. God's invitation to intimacy is, wonderfully, given to us all.

The spiritual opportunity is universal. Thus, George Fox had no claim to spiritual authority above any other Quaker. He had no special or particular relationship with God but in his moment of brokenness, of openness, discovered God's wonderful, ongoing and fulsome invitation to the whole of humanity. This is an invitation that in its direct and inward nature steers us away from unhelpful adulation of others or pride within. Simply, we are called to be faithful vessels of God's loving ministry, one to another.

We all are blessed with gifts to help further God's loving purposes, we all have a ministry. Our sense of vocation may be life-long or be made up of a series of new calls. "I know I'm a teacher, that's my ministry. But that's not the only gift or ministry I have . . . I'm waiting for an answer as to what is next . . . in the form of an opening." We can be called like Mary without any sense of choice, or like Moses where there appeared to be choice, or be offered a genuine choice by God, or discover, delightfully, that we are already living our call: "I used to wonder what I was going to be when I grew up. I spent three years on a quest to find out . . . it finally occurred to me that the life I'm in right now is my ministry. Surrendering is not an intellectual experience. When I finally was able to let go, I realised the life I'm living was it . . . it is unbelievably exciting to surrender and let life take me where it will." We are not to be shy of the power and authority of the gifts we are given but joyfully surrender to the life we are called to lead, and use those gifts humbly and obediently.

We are all invited into the corporate encounter with God. In traditional Christian terms, we are all saved, all loved. Equally, we are all responsible, all part of the corporate priesthood realising God's kingdom in all we do and say. "It's taken me a long time to understand how sitting in prayer or contemplation *among* other people is different from sitting in prayer or contemplation *with* other people." The Quaker way is not to be lived apart. We enact our faith, called to a life of justice, compassion, joy and prayerful attention amongst our community and amidst the challenges of the everyday. God calls us, all of us, directly. Our role is to respond.

2 Worship

We call the grace we are given to respond to God "that of God in everyone". It is not about God being within all, but about the ability to experience God within and in turn to take up our part in the priesthood. "In meeting, if I can silence my ego, my stuff, I can actually hear – and in the hearing, connect to others. When I can be present, I feel God's presence."

Living out our faith as a 'priesthood of all believers' gives us options when it comes to worship. We could ask the person with a gift of nurturing worship to take that role on for us (akin to Quaker pastors in the majority of the Quaker world, or elders), or we could rotate the leadership of worship week by week. However, the reliability of silence and stillness, the direct inward nature of divine leadership we regularly experience, and the fact that we are all ministers, has led us for over 350 years to employ and enjoy 'open' or 'unprogrammed' worship and a 'free ministry'. In other words, we choose worship based in silence without rite or rote, with words (vocal ministry) only shared when *any* one of us feels led to offer them.

The first consequence of this is that there is no 'front' to a Quaker meeting as there is no one or no-thing to face. Typically we worship in a circle or a square denoting how we come before the Holy Other as equals, each with our shortcomings and our skills, frustrated hopes and wildest dreams, our longing for God. Second, there is no need for anything to be said or done outwardly. We simply surrender ourselves to experience, the play of God's Light on the depths of our being. Silence and stillness nurture the sense of presence, and anything that is spoken is to add to the riches we find in the silence. Third, in that place of encounter and transformation, we are called to discern whether what we feel led to share is really ministry. Is this a message from God or a response to somebody else's ministry? Is it repetition? Is it a bright idea? Is it only about me? If it is a message from God, is it to be shared outwardly? With this group? At this time? Through me? If yes, we need to faithfully relay what we have been given. Sometimes, whilst we are still discerning, someone else is on their feet expressing the very sentiments we had been given, or the moment clearly passes and we were rightly silent.

&#x03;

So, worship begins in quiet, the silence tending the stilling and the stilling tending the silence. Friends have different ways into the silence, of 'centring down'. Some of us start by praying for everyone else there, others of us follow a personal meditation to help move us across from all our thoughts and concerns, and still others of us find it possible to simply sink into the silence, to 'keep low' and withdraw from our selves before God. Practice helps. Silence is not easy but also cannot be feigned: in the midst of divine encounter, we know when we are there. When the whole group reaches that place, the meeting is called 'gathered' or 'covered'. As we become practised at worship, so we get more and more from these intentional moments of corporate response to God's loving invitation. "The experience of other silences is not the same . . . Quaker silence is different. It brings peace."

When we are given ministry to share, we typically stand to offer it so as to be better heard and to help us remember what we are about; the free ministry is potentially risky and Quaker writers have talked about "the dangers of silent worship": we could easily fill worship with talk or good ideas and turn our back on the Divine or crowd God out. To nurture our expectant waiting, we leave spaces between ministry to reflect on what has been shared, avoid speaking right at the beginning or right at the end, and only minister once in a meeting. God may give us much to say but we are encouraged to distil it into as few words as possible or let it mature for a future meeting. In large meetings, we are encouraged to remain silent if we are unsure if what we have to say is really ministry. In smaller meetings, perhaps hungry for vocal ministry to help feed the discipline of our inward communion, we might say "If in doubt, do!" My own small meeting often starts with a reading to help us towards the attention we need to give to quieting ourselves before God, and to encourage vocal ministry.

We are given ministry by grace to share freely. It may be helpful to some but not all and it is not for us to judge it. As ministry is not discussion or response, so it does not lead to discussion or response. Most people are clear when they have shared ministry and some find themselves on their feet before they are aware of very much at all. "I feel a leading – whether to speak in meeting or something larger – first as a funny internal wiggle that eventually grows into a full body awareness. Sometimes when I become totally clear and follow a leading I may cry a bit because it's so powerful."

We appoint elders from amongst us to help nurture our worship, to encourage ministry from the tentative, and to remind us if we minister when things were better left unsaid. On rare occasions, elders interrupt a long ministry to help restore the silence for the rest of the group. It is a difficult step to take as ministry is, in theory, divinely inspired and the elders need to practise their own discernment whether or not to act.

Elders 'close' or end worship by shaking hands. In the past half-century, everyone has taken to following this lead. We greet each other, welcome each other back into the world, and give thanks for the worship we have shared and the community we feel part of. Worship is typically an hour but may extend if there is much ministry or ministry right at the end. Time is only outward and ending worship at a particular time is far less important than being open to the winds of the Spirit.

The same discipline applies to our meetings for worship for marriage or to give thanks for the life of a departed Friend. We witness to what God is giving to us inwardly in the silence and outwardly through vocal ministry. The outward is a reflection of the inward spiritual reality. Our outward expression reflects what God is realising, making real, in, through, and amongst us, whether it be a call to action, gratitude for a faithful life, or the marriage by God of two of our number. The dynamic heart of all of our meetings is inward encounter and outward expression, the recognition, celebration and outworking of all that is given by God.

∽

Discernment is central to the Quaker way. Without the mediation of text or minister, we need to work out for ourselves what is and what is not of God. Discernment is the key discipline to accompany the claim that God's guidance is available to us all individually, the responsibility that accompanies the gift of grace. Like silence, it is something we work on and develop our skills in. We need to 'test' what is given us, in and through our own spiritual experience but also in and through the spiritual experience of others in our community. This is not always possible and we may only realise the faithfulness of an action retrospectively – the rush of energy, the flow of positive consequences like a row of falling dominoes, or the fruits of the Spirit that follow a rightly led decision or the opposite for one that was not. We discern if and when to minister in meeting, elders discern when to act in meeting, and we may hold a 'clearness meeting' to discern with others whether we are truly led and 'clear' to marry, or whether or not to take a new job. We are not necessarily seeking answers but we are trying to know what it is to be faithful, what it means to be true to the Spirit.

"About five years ago I went to a monastery and ran into a Benedictine monk who'd been there for sixty years. I asked him how he discerned, how he sought the will of God. He said, 'I don't . . . ask for guidance. I don't pray. It's just there.' . . . He was just living it out . . . Being in the silence has been challenging for me, but there's an inner observer there that . . . shines a light on my more selfish tendencies."

As a people continually open to and led by the Spirit, we are continually discerning. Without discernment, our discipleship fails, our worship fails and we are left with only a secular shadow. We need to be open to God and prepared to wrestle with the temptations of our own imaginations.

03

When we engage with our meetings for business or 'church affairs', we are involved in a discernment process based in worship. In traditional Quaker terms, we are seeking the will of God. In the past decades this phrase has been variously interpreted, as Quaker theology has become more diverse. For some Friends, 'God' is an unhelpful term or they believe in a God that does not have a will. For others, 'will' means different things, ranging from where God has an answer to every question, to broad brush preferences whereby we are left to sort out the detail. For others, God learns as we do and God's will is co-created. Whatever our theology of God's will, we know we best find the way forward by entering into worship.

We appoint a 'clerk' to help us maintain our discipline in meetings for worship for business, although elders also nurture the worship and support 'the table'. The clerk does not lead but 'serves', helping us remember our process and what we are about. We worship, pray, and listen for divine nudgings and promptings and when led, we rise to offer ministry to help the meeting forward. In larger gatherings, more than one Friend may stand at the same time and the clerk discerns who to 'call'. As with all vocal ministry, our spoken contributions are usually short and concise. Silence ensues before another ministry is prompted, another of us called. Contributions are addressed to the clerk and as in all worship, this is not a time for conversation or discussion. We are involved in a God-guided process, not a task. We are not engaged in finding a solution to a problem but seeking to know what God is calling us to at this time. The clerk's role is to discern the 'sense of the meeting' based on the ministry and to record this in a 'minute'. The clerk prepares and reads a draft of the minute when they feel the time is right and the discernment continues on the minute, no longer the matter. "I love to clerk business meetings – I find Jesus Christ sitting next to me. It gives me phenomenal courage to get out of the way. It is so not like me to have Jesus Christ in my life. That is when I am most aware of the Divine, when I am most trusting, when I am at my best."

The clerk drafts the minute and asks "Is the minute acceptable?" and if it is 'good enough', we reply "Hope so". Personally, we hope it is, and collectively, we hope we have discerned correctly. None of us claim to know God's will so well as to call out "Yes!" The minute is only accepted if everyone or virtually everyone is in agreement or agrees to agree. This may mean that if a few of us cannot agree on a minute, the decision does not go ahead.

As God's will is seen to be singular, so finding the sense of the meeting on an item is seen to represent a rightly discerned decision. We do not vote on business items and not being in unity may tell us the discernment is not complete. Sometimes a small minority hold out for a decision that eventually the large body comes to see is 'in right ordering' (in God's ordering). As a religious society, the decision may not be the most rational, logical or even outwardly sensible, but it is what we hope and believe God wants us to do. I remember a Friend rising and saying: "If we were the Society of Friends I would oppose this proposal as risky and irrational but we are the Religious Society of Friends and I am feeling strongly led that we should accept this proposal." Yearly Meeting in session is regularly inspiring. Gatherings of over one thousand Friends finding the sense of the meeting on a difficult issue is always affirming of our ability to enact our discipleship and discern faithfully. "Most of my experiences of God at work have been in big meetings for worship for business. You feel it, you know. While we've done our homework and preparation on a subject, the timing is unexpected. This happened with the issue of gay and lesbian unions in our meeting. Suddenly Friends were moving into unity. There's an amazing joy, the feeling of the

Spirit filling the room and spreading out to all those in our community beyond those present in the room. Surprise and joy are the hallmarks for me of God's guidance. It feels right."

We are not to know where we may be led and we may come to see that our hopes were for things way beyond our imagination. "There are God-incidents (not coincidences) in life. Something is at work through life. The common pattern is being surprised . . . and grateful." What is important is being faithful to the next step and knowing we take it not in our power but in God's.

$$\text{cg}$$

Our structure, and the way of doing business through the testing of leadings, is largely unchanged from the early Quaker vision of 'Gospel Order'. In other words, our system of 'church government' reflects how we feel God wants the Quaker Church to be organised. It is a decentralised pattern with most decisions taken locally. Each meeting is based on a flat structure; we are levelled down before the leadership of God or the Spirit.

As a group focused on the inward encounter, all of the outward forms of worship are to some extent pragmatic. Some habits, like the recent practice of having flowers on the table in the middle, have no theological logic, they simply appeal. Some meetings experiment with all-age worship where the children and young people stay and contribute to the meeting rather than attending 'children's class'. Others experiment with untimed worship or meetings lasting three hours as they used to. Some have abandoned all local committees when faced with difficulty filling them and reworked their volunteering around their most pressing needs. Some, keen to reduce their carbon footprint, now meet on Saturdays instead of Sundays so Friends have access to better public transport. Quakerism is our attempt at collective congruity with the workings of the Spirit and it can change as it needs to. The future of how we practise our faith lies in all of our hands and hearts, in our collective discernment. There is no 'they' in Quakerism, only 'us', and we are all learning all the time, open to new Light, continuing to seek along the spiritual path we call the Quaker way. Wonderfully, we regularly find the totally unexpected and the totally amazing, such are its abundant riches.

3   Life

Our spiritual experience draws us closer to God. When we experience intimacy with the Divine, we are given a sense of God that is beyond words and beyond full understanding. Whilst earlier generations of Quakers were very sure about what they believed, we are clear that we cannot be wholly or finally sure about doctrine. We each make sense of our spiritual experience but we do not imagine that the way we understand the holy is necessarily right for anyone else. We are sure for ourselves or sure partially or sure provisionally, for now, but not sure completely or for everyone or for all time. Paradoxically, we feel pretty certain about this at-least partial uncertainty. In this way, our beliefs are 'towards' or 'perhaps' kind of ones and we are cautious about anyone who claims they have the final word of God or can totally understand God and God's ways. "It is possible to be open and ardent at the same time. Too often, those who are ardent are closed off. To be open as a Quaker one has to listen. Your meeting holds your feet to the fire. It's the only place I've found this connection."

Our open worship accommodates our theological diversity. We agree how to worship and how to do business, in other words how to make space to experience God. We are also clear that speaking of religious belief always falls short because the words we have never match the depth of that experience. Quakers have never adopted a creed. Quaker faith is revealed by our lives, not language. We minister in different theological dialects and become adept at translating the meaning of the ministry into our own spiritual language, or of feeling beyond and behind it. "When I started going to meeting, I kept wanting to go back. Becoming part of the community was like a promise to myself. It was a spiritual promise to search and be part of a community. Being surrounded by those people has been a huge blessing that has changed my life . . . has brought me to a real faith. Just reading books about spirituality would not have brought me to the same place. It wouldn't have happened." The Quaker way is not about profession but possession. We let our lives preach.

 C33

The idea of "that of God in everyone" and the spiritual equality that accompanies this idea of the universal elect means that everyone is equally important. Each of us is a unique and precious child of God. Thus, we have always opposed killing and war and anything which diminishes another. Our witness, our testimony, is the way we live because spiritually we can do no other. "When I left the Protestant Church, I was looking for simplicity, peace and equality. I needed those." Our tradition and practice encourages and affirms us to lead a spiritual life embedded in how God is calling us to live. "The work that I do is with people. When we connect, we grow God in the world." We become testimony.

We are less wary of 'the world' than the earlier Friends. They wore Quaker grey as a plain form of dress, refused to use the pagan names for days and months or use titles or the deferential 'you', preferring 'thee' and 'thou'. In their levelling of society, they eschewed worldly manners such as bowing or the doffing of a hat. They outlawed for themselves music and theatre and novels. They refused to pay tithes to the "hireling ministry" or swear in court because of the injunction in the book of Matthew's gospel not to swear and because they said they told the truth all of the time. We still affirm in court but have become freer about how we dress and also about music and the arts, feeling we can maintain our integrity inwardly and enjoy these outward forms. We are less worried about emotions and 'self' getting in the way of our relationship to God than our forebears. We have translated the ideal of plainness into simplicity and being 'against war' into being 'for peace'. We are more relaxed about 'marrying out' (marrying a non-Quaker), which led to thousands leaving Quakerism. Indeed, many of us are now married to or in partnership with non-Quakers and in the last one hundred years a dynastic and familial Quakerism has been replaced by 85 per cent of us becoming Friends as adults. We are very clear we want to be engaged with the world and that our faith needs to be relevant to the age.

Early Quakers did not have a membership system; it was obvious by dress and speech who was and who was not a Quaker. In the 1730s, British Quakers made up lists to work out which meeting would give poor relief to which Quaker families and, by default, 'membership lists' were created. Children were automatically listed as members until 1959. Today, people apply for membership as it helps them be clear to themselves and the world that they are Quakers. It denotes no greater spiritual development or maturity but is a public statement of saying we understand the Quaker way and are committed to it. It is about being part of the priesthood and sharing the service that our collective work and worship requires. "It's not being a member that's important, it is what being a member stands for." At the same time, everyone is equal before God and, members or not, we are a single community of worshippers bound together by the riches of all we experience and the desire to discern how we are to live our faith. "I've found [in Quaker meeting] . . . a sense of being held, and it seems authentic."

However, alongside a more relaxed approach to how and who we are, we are also clear that there is much about modern consumer culture that we cannot support or participate in. We work for a more just and peaceful world, one with less discrimination and greater equality, a more sustainable approach to the economy and to the planet, and a greater degree of integrity amongst those entrusted with power and responsibility. We feel these certainties deeply, beyond conscious choice. These values are who we are. They affect what we buy and where we shop, how or if we travel, how we are in the workplace. We try not to be dissuaded from doing the right thing just because it is unpopular. We are active in all kinds of organisations to try to achieve these ends, not in our own power, but based on the holy imperatives given us in worship. We care passionately.

Knowing how to act and when calls for discernment. Some moral dilemmas are not easy. Do we hide refugees facing death even if it means lying to the authorities? How far can we maintain our testimony against violence and killing if our families are threatened? We cannot say until faced with the situation and we have taken individual paths as we have felt led. Thus, we do not agree on everything. We have different views on alcohol or the lottery. Some have difficulty with pacifism, and in the two World Wars many individuals joined up whilst others went to prison as conscientious objectors. Each of us is called to try to discern the right course and we can ask little more of each other than the sincere attempt to get it as right as we can, to keep discerning. We need each other to help test our different leadings and to be here for each other when we get things wrong, as we do and will: we are not Quakers together because we are 'good' but because we are not. "Quakers need to be in community for fellowship, decision-making and support."

We share a strongly felt optimism about humanity and human potential and with it an overwhelming compassion for each other and the rest of humanity, our neighbours in the widest sense. "I grew up in a Quaker family. There was a feeling that there was a lot to be thankful for. I learned to be kind to the animals. It wasn't difficult to attend meeting. It was a way of life around the farm." We are called to help create a loving society.

C3

Our spiritual experience leads us to new levels or inward sites of spiritual relationship which are continuous. George Fox talked about being taken through "the flaming sword" back into the Garden of Eden and other early Friends talked of being made anew. In a less dramatic way, I have felt God's accompaniment in my life daily since that day I was unexpectedly lifted out of my seat on the Greyhound bus, held, and encouraged towards a new life by what has been a very patient teacher! We keep trying to live the faithful life and we keep learning the faithful life.

My experience of an accompanied life is not true for everyone but we are clear that a life of trying to live God's loving purposes is not limited to the Sunday morning or midweek meeting. We are called to witness to those purposes all of the time, to help the kingdom unfold in the here and now. Early Quakers never developed a theology of the afterlife because they never imagined they needed one: they had such a strong sense of the world being turned upside down in the 1650s that the New Jerusalem would be realised in their lifetime. The world did not change as much as they imagined and 'Gospel Order' and the building of meeting houses from the 1670s was one consequence of realising it was a longer journey.

The witness of our everyday lives continues and is continuous, but we feel the urgency to transform the world as keenly as our forebears.

Quaker silence always has consequences. The inward leads to the outward. As we listen to what God is calling us to, there will always be more to know and more to realise, make real. Faithful living is always an ongoing process, a joyful and necessarily continuous witness to the expression of God's love for all of humanity. "God is not 'encounters' for me, it's something right there over my shoulder and accessible at any time."

We may travel to the historic Quaker sites to get a better sense of the first years of Quakerism but no place is any more sacred than any other: we do not have a theology of pilgrimage. Rather, everywhere is a 'thin place' where we can connect with the majesty of mystical experience. Similarly, all times are equally special and we meet when it is convenient to do so. Early Quakers were criticised for opening their shops on Christmas Day. Today, some of us celebrate Christmas but no day is more sacred than any other. Every day is Christmas and Easter, such is the power, reach and continuity of our intimacy with God. "I feel that God or the Spirit is my constant companion – that I am accompanied, surrounded." We live in God's time.

୯ଌ

Early Quakers had a mission to the world. They felt they were the true Church and everyone could be and needed to be saved. The kingdom of heaven was to be realised on earth. British Quakers today talk little of salvation but we maintain a sense of outreach to everyone, a present-day version of our good news. "I have no reservations about the good news of Quakerism. There are lots of people looking for what we have to offer. The Quaker way lets people experience God directly, letting everyone take responsibility for their spiritual growth." We have a unique approach to worship and to the nature of religious belief, a particular understanding of connection with God and of being a people of God. We have a key focus on discerning what God is calling us to do and proven methods for realising that collective seeking, and a strong set of spiritual values aimed at making the world a better place for all of creation.

We live the Quaker way. Every day. We are the Quaker way.

Reflection and discussion

The following questions are designed to help you reflect on your own experience of what you value, celebrate and understand for yourself about the Quaker way.

They can be used either for individual reflection, or by small groups.

If you are meeting as a group, agree some ground rules at the beginning. Important ones might be to allow everyone a chance to speak, to speak only from your own experience, and that no one has to speak if they don't want to.

Make sure that the book and the questions are accessible to anyone not able to read print, either by obtaining an audio version or reading relevant sections aloud in the group.

If the group is large, you may wish to spend some time in twos, threes or fours before returning to the large group.

Choose between worship sharing or group discussion. Groups may prefer one or the other. Some dislike the discipline of worship sharing when they are bursting with ideas; some find it difficult to contribute in a discussion if they are not given a specific space to do so. Be sensitive to everyone's needs.

Questions for reflection and discussion

1. Inward spirituality
    a) Think of moments when the Spirit has been at work in your life or when you have felt closest to the Divine. What was it like? Is there any pattern?
    b) What are your gifts? What is your ministry?
    c) How do you nurture your spirituality?
    d) What does the Quaker way give you?

2. Worship
    a) What is your experience of worship? What words do you use to describe it?
    b) How do you make decisions in your life? Does anyone from meeting help you?
    c) What are business meetings like in your meeting? Is there anything you would like to change?
    d) What helps you discern?

3. Life
    a) Do you do anything differently as a consequence of attending Quaker meeting?
    b) Does coming to Quaker meeting help you in your life? If so, how? Do you feel supported by your meeting in the choices you make?
    c) What is your vision for Quakerism? How are we going to get there?
    d) What is the good news about Quakerism for you? What do you want to tell others about?

9 781907 123276